LET'S·READ·AND·FIND·OUT SCIENCE®

What Makes a Shadow?

REVISED EDITION

By Clyde Robert Bulla

Illustrated by June Otani

SCHOLASTIC INC.
New York Toronto London Auckland Sydney

The *Let's-Read-and-Find-Out Science* book series was originated by Dr. Franklyn M. Branley, Astronomer Emeritus and former Chairman of the American Museum–Hayden Planetarium, and was formerly co-edited by him and Dr. Roma Gans, Professor Emeritus of Childhood Education, Teachers College, Columbia University. Text and illustrations for each of the books in the series are checked for accuracy by an expert in the relevant field. For a complete catalog of Let's-Read-and-Find-Out Science books, write to HarperCollins Children's Books, 10 East 53rd Street, New York, NY 10022.

Let's-Read-and-Find-Out Science® is a trademark of HarperCollins Publishers Inc.

ISBN 0-590-27593-3

12 11 10 9 8 7 6 5 4 3   8 9/9 0 1 2 3/0

Printed in the U.S.A.   08

First Scholastic printing, January 1998

What Makes a Shadow?

The sun is shining. It shines on the trees and the sidewalk. It shines on your house.
It shines on you, too.

When the sun is in front of you, look behind you. You can see your shadow. When you move, your shadow moves. When you run, your shadow runs. But you can never catch it.

What makes the shadow? Where does it come from?

The sun is very bright. It shines on the house. It shines on the trees. It shines on you. But the sun does not shine *through* you.

There is a dark place behind you where the sun does not shine. The darkness is your shadow.

Look for more shadows.

A tree has a shadow. The shade of the tree is the shadow of the tree.

A house has a shadow.

The sun shines on one side of the house. There is a shadow on the other side.

Animals have shadows.

So do cars.

Airplanes have shadows. Watch as an airplane flies
over your head. You may see its shadow on the ground.

A cloud has a shadow.

Sometimes the sky is dark with clouds. The sun cannot shine through them. The shadows of the clouds fall on the earth. The shadows make the day dark. We say, "This is a cloudy day."

Some shadows are darker than others. Hold a paper towel so the sun shines on it. The paper towel makes a shadow on the ground. The shadow is not dark because some of the sunlight shines through.

Hold a book so the sun shines on it. The book makes a
shadow on the ground. It makes a dark shadow because
no sunlight shines through.

Watch the sun go down.

Watch the night come.

Night is a shadow.

The sun shines on one side of the earth. The other side is in shadow. The shadow makes the night.

Inside the house at night you can see more shadows. Hold your hand between a lamp and the wall. You will see the shadow of your hand on the wall.

Do you know how to make a big shadow?

Hold your hand close to the lamp, but not too close. The light bulb may be hot! The shadow is big because your hand shuts out so much of the light. This makes more darkness on the wall.

Move your hand away from the light. Move it farther and farther away. Now the shadow on the wall gets smaller and smaller and smaller. It is smaller because your hand does not shut out so much light. There is less darkness on the wall.

You can have fun with shadows. Hold your hands between
the light and the wall and make shadow pictures. You can make a
duck. Or a dog. Or a rabbit.

You can make shadow pictures little or big. You can move
your hands to make the pictures move.

There are other shadow pictures you can make. Here are some.

Look for shadows. How many can you find?

When you find shadows, see if you can discover what makes each one.

30